MY HOPE FOR AMERICA

MY HOPE FOR AMERICA

by Lyndon B. Johnson

RANDOM HOUSE • NEW YORK

CONTENTS

PREFACE

When I was young I often walked out at night and looked at the scattered Texas sky.

As a boy in those still nights I wondered what those heavens had seen, what they would see, and what they might bring to me.

The world has turned many times since then.

But still, at evening, I sometimes look across the great city where I live and dream the same dreams and ask the same questions.

Just as most people do, I sit and think of today's events and tomorrow's problems. I feel glad in my family and concerned for my children.

It is then I remember the men who captured my native soil from the wilderness. They endured much so that others might have much. Their dream was for the children. Mine, too, is for the child even now struggling toward birth.

What will the observing sky say of the world we have built for him?

I want all the ages of man to yield him their promise.

The child will find all knowledge open to him.

The growing boy will shape his spirit in a house of God, and his ways in the house of his family.

The young man will find reward for his work, and feel pride in the product of his skills.

The man will find leisure an occasion for the closeness of family, and an opportunity for the enrichment of life.

The citizen will enrich the nation—sharing its rule, walking its streets, adding his views to its counsel—secure always from the unjust and arbitrary power of his fellows.

The least among us will find contentment, and the best among us can find greatness. All of us will respect the dignity of the one and admire the achievements of the other.

At the end of the journey he will look back and say: I have done all a man could do—built all, shared all, experienced all.

And man shall say to man: There, on this earth as in the eyes of God, walks my brother.

This is my dream.

It is not the grand vision of a powerful and feared nation. It concerns the simple wants of people.

But this is what America is all about.

All the rest—the power and wealth, the life of freedom and the hopes for peace, the treasured past and the uncertain future—will stand or fall on this.

Reality rarely matches dream. But only dreams give nobility to purpose.

This is the star I hope to follow—which I know most of you have seen, and which I first glimpsed many years ago in the Texas night.

1

PRESIDENT OF ALL THE PEOPLE

"A tragic twist of fateful sorrow made me President. From that awful day on November 22nd, when President Kennedy was assassinated, I have had but one thought, but one conviction, but one objective: To be the President of all the people, not just the rich, not just the well fed, not just the fortunate, but President of all America."

One of the hardest tasks a President faces is to keep the time scale of his decisions always in mind. He is not simply responsible to an immediate electorate. He knows how great can be the repercussions of all that he does or that he fails to do. The President always has to think of America as a continuing community. He has to try to see how his decisions will affect not only today's citizens but their children and their children's children. He has to try to peer into the future, and he has to prepare for that future.

If the policies he advocates lack this dimension of depth and this dimension of staying power, he may gain advantage in the short run, but he can set the country on a wrong course.

The President of this country, more than any other man in the world, must grapple with the course of events and the directions of history. What he must try to do is to build for tomorrow in the immediacy of today. Somehow, he must ignite a fire in the breast of this land, a flaming spirit of adventure that soars beyond the ordinary and the contented, demanding greatness from our society and achievement in our government.

I have felt a deep interest in studying the American Presidency ever since Franklin D. Roosevelt first brought me into the White House when I was only twenty-seven. The Nation has been blessed with strong and popular and successful Presidents. But the emphasis upon the individuals has caused us to neglect our understanding of the office itself. If the Presidency is to serve the people in these times as they want to be served, we need the fullest appreciation of the powers and the limitations of that office.

Back in 1900 Admiral Dewey said he was convinced that "the office of the President is not such a very difficult one to fill." I doubt that was true even in 1900. I know it is not true today. This office is a difficult office, and anyone who occupies it must be a humble man. The office towers above the man and gives him strength that is much greater than his own.

The Presidency of this Nation is no place for a timid soul or a torpid spirit. The basic freedoms—the world that Franklin Roosevelt envisioned and that John Kennedy worked and died for—have taken on new meaning in our time. They are a part of our heritage. And from that heritage the President must draw the goals and the guidance best suited for his own time.

He must be determined to preserve in the future what we have received from the past. But he also must be aware that only by accepting the arduous, uncertain, and very lonely duty of interpreting democracy according to the needs of today—only then can he hope that posterity will say, "He, too, guarded and handed on the Great Experiment."

A tragic twist of fateful sorrow made me President. From that awful day on November 22nd, when President Kennedy was assassinated, I have had but one thought, but one conviction, but one objective: To be the President of all the people, not just the rich, not just the well fed, not just the fortunate, but President of all America.

Every day there come to this office new problems and new crises and new difficulties demanding discussion and consultation and decision. I must deal with them, possessing no gift of prophecy, no special insight into history. Instead, I must depend, as my thirty-five predecessors have depended, on the best wisdom and judgment that can be summoned to the service of the Nation. This counsel must come from people who represent the diversity of America.

A President must have a vision of the America and the world he wants to see. But the President does not put his purely personal stamp upon the future. His vision is compounded of the hopes and anxieties and values of the people he serves. The President can help guide them toward the highest and most noble of their desires. He cannot take them where they do not want to go. Nor can he hope to move ahead without the help of all those who share a common purpose. I believe the Presidency was conceived as an office of persuasion more than of sheer power. That is how I have tried to use the office since it was thrust upon me.

Our land often sounds too many discordant notes. There are the voices of those who seek to divide our purpose and to separate our people. But the din of these voices must not fool us into believing that we live in a divided nation.

I have traveled to every part of this country, and one thing is clear to me: The farmer in Iowa, the fisherman in Massachusetts, the worker in Seattle, and the rancher in Texas have the same hopes and harbor the same fears. They want education for their children and an improving life for their families. They want to protect liberty and they want to pursue peace. They expect justice for themselves and they are willing to grant it to others.

This is the real voice of America. And it is one of the great tasks of Presidential leadership to make our people aware that they share a fundamental unity of interest and purpose and belief.

I am going to try to accomplish this. I intend to try to achieve a broad national consensus which can end obstruction and paralysis, and which can liberate the energies of the Nation for the work of the future.

I truly believe that someday we will see an America that knows no North or South, no East or West—an America undivided by creed or color, untorn by suspicion or strife.

17

· · ·

I want a people who are fearless instead of fearful; men with pride in their ancestry and hope for their posterity, humble before their God and concerned always with the wants as well as the needs of their fellow human beings. For in a democracy, high purpose, no matter how nobly conceived, must surely fail without the understanding and the unity of the people.

2

A PRESIDENT'S FAITH
AND VISION

"One hundred years ago, Lincoln told us that this Nation could not stand half-slave and half-free. For my part, I believe this society cannot succeed part committed and part uncommitted, part concerned and part unconcerned, part compassionate and part callous."

In the long view of history, these years of the 1960s are the early summer of America. Our land is young. Our strength is great. Our course is far from run.

Yet, there is among our people a deep discontent. Why? It seems to me we can find answers from our history. In our national character, one trait has run unbroken. That is the trait of putting the resources at hand to the fullest use—to make life better. Americans have, as De Tocqueville said of us, "A lively faith in the perfectibility of man. . . . They admit that what appears to them today to be good, may be superseded by something better tomorrow."

. . .

Since World War II, we have multiplied our capabilities as never before, but we have not put them to the fullest use. We have the capacity to abolish hunger. We have the capacity to end poverty and to eliminate most diseases. We even have the capacity to unsnarl our traffic.

But we have not put these capacities to work. Our cities show it. Our schools show it. Our rural areas show it. Our rivers and streams show it. The edges of our society show it.

We are engaged in a breakneck race toward discovery. In the next twenty-four hours the research that comes forth around the world would fill seven sets of the *Encyclopaedia Britannica*. In the next year the output of such research would require a man to read around the clock—day and night—for the next 460 years. In the next ten years the sum of human knowledge will multiply twofold.

When knowledge is advancing at this pace, a compassionate nation cannot afford to leave any segments of our society behind to form and to perpetuate a human slag heap. In our private lives as in our public policies we are challenged to show compassion. When the helpless call for help—the hearing must hear, the seeing must see, and the able must act.

. . .

One hundred years ago, Lincoln told us that this Nation could not stand half-slave and half-free. For my part, I believe this society cannot succeed part committed and part uncommitted, part concerned and part unconcerned, part compassionate and part callous.

The ultimate test of our civilization, the ultimate test of our faithfulness to our past, is not in our goods or our guns. It is in the quality of our peoples' lives and in the character of the men and women our society produces.

The contest is the same that men have faced at every turning point in history. It is not between liberals and conservatives; it is not between party and party, or platform and platform. It is between courage and timidity. It is between those who have vision and who see what can be and those who want only to maintain the status quo. It is between those who welcome the future and those who turn away from its promise.

The man who is hungry—who cannot find work or educate his children—that man is not fully free. For more than thirty years, from Social Security to the war against poverty, we have worked diligently to enlarge the freedom of man. And as a result, more Americans than ever before are free to live as they want to live, to pursue their ambitions, to meet their desires, to raise their families. But the task is not finished.

I believe it is one of the strengths of the United States that we have never had a single, rigid ideology. We do have deep beliefs for which millions have fought and died. All of our efforts and our hopes are directed to securing a world in which men can live for their beliefs rather than die for them.

But these are beliefs in man's right to freedom, to the good life, to spiritual fulfillment. They are beliefs which concern the hopes of people; they are not systems of thought which strike at the dreams of the individual in the name of the state or in the arrogant belief that a single man or group of men can prophesy the demands of history.

The variety of human experience cannot be contained in a single law or a single system or a single belief. We cannot make experience conform to dogma. No man or nation is wise enough to prescribe a single economic system or a single set of political institutions to meet the needs of more than a hundred countries, each with its own history, its own resources, its own culture, and its own proud spiritual tradition. Each must be free to seek its own destiny in its own way.

We know how hard it is to explain democracy. One of our great poets, Carl Sandburg, sensed this when he wrote, "Of course, we can't answer the question what is democracy smoothly and easily like we answer 'where is the railroad station or which way is the post office.'"

To some, who have been numbed by the magnitude of the challenges we face, the prospects for democracy are hopeless. Only recently a man came to see me in the White House and said, "Nothing we do will help. The population explosion is submerging our cities in a sea of futility. The harder we work, the more there is to do."

I feel sorry for that man. I feel sorry for any American who has lost faith in the capacity of the American people. I feel sorry for the country, too, when even one citizen loses hope. For while we stand on the very edge of a great society, timid dreams and faint resolve will never help us to achieve it.

I am not a theologian. I am not a philosopher. I am just a public servant doing the very best I know how. But in more than three decades of public life, I have seen first-hand that basic spiritual beliefs can shatter barriers of bias and bigotry. From this experience I have drawn new hope that the seemingly insurmountable issues we face at home and abroad can be resolved by men of strong faith and men of brave deeds.

Lincoln proclaimed as a national faith that right makes might. Surely this is so, and surely if we are to complete the great unfinished work of our society, spiritual beliefs from which social actions spring must be the strongest weapons in our arsenal.

3

THE CHALLENGES OF JUSTICE

"The Civil Rights Act is a challenge to men of good will to transform the commands of our law into the customs of our land."

One hundred and eighty-eight years ago a small band of valiant men began a long struggle for freedom. They pledged their lives, their fortunes, and their sacred honor, not only to found a nation, but to forge an ideal of freedom; not only for political independence, but for personal liberty; not only to eliminate foreign rule, but to establish the rule of justice in the affairs of men.

That struggle was a turning point in our history. Today in far corners of distant continents, the ideals of those American patriots still shape the struggles of men who hunger for freedom.

•   •   ○

This is a proud triumph. Yet those who founded our country knew that freedom would be secure only if each generation fought to renew and enlarge its meaning. From the Minutemen at Concord to the soldiers in Vietnam, each generation has been equal to that trust.

Americans of every race and color have died in battle to protect our freedom. Americans of every race and color have worked to build a nation of widening opportunities. Now our generation of Americans has been called on to continue the unending search for justice within our own borders.

We believe that all men are created equal. Yet many are denied equal treatment. We believe that all men have certain unalienable rights. Yet many Americans do not enjoy those rights. We believe that all men are entitled to the blessings of liberty. Yet millions are being deprived of those blessings— not because of their own failures, but because of the color of their skins.

The reasons are deeply imbedded in history and tradition and the nature of man. We can understand—without rancor or hatred—how all this happened.

But it cannot continue. Our Constitution, the foundation of our Republic, forbids it. The principles of our freedom forbid it. Morality forbids it. And now the law forbids it.

That law is the product of the most careful debate and discussion. It was proposed by our late and beloved President, John F. Kennedy. It received the bipartisan support of more than two thirds of the members of both the House and Senate. An overwhelming majority of Republicans as well as Democrats voted for it. It has received the thoughtful support of tens of thousands of civic and religious leaders in all parts of this Nation. And it is supported by the great majority of the American people.

The purpose of the law is simple. It does not restrict the freedom of any American so long as he respects the rights of others. It does not give special treatment to any citizen.

It does say that those who are equal before God shall also be equal in the polling booths, in the classrooms, in the factories, and in hotels, restaurants, movie theaters, and other places that provide service to the public.

We do not approach the observance and enforcement of this law in a vengeful spirit. Its purpose is not to punish. Its purpose is not to divide, but to end divisions—divisions which have lasted all too long. Its purpose is national, not regional. Its purpose is to promote a more abiding commitment to freedom, a more constant pursuit of justice, and a deeper respect for human dignity.

No single act of Congress can, by itself, eliminate discrimination and prejudice, hatred and injustice. But this act goes further to invest the rights of man with the protection of law than any legislation in this entire century.

First, it provides a code carefully designed to test and enforce the right of every American to go to school, for every American to get a job, for every American to vote and to pursue his life unhampered by the barriers of racial discrimination.

Second, it educates all Americans to the responsibility to give equal treatment to their fellow citizens.

Third, it enlists one of the most powerful moral forces of American society on the side of civil rights —the moral obligation to respect and obey the law of the land.

Fourth, and perhaps most important, this act is a renewal and a reinforcement, a symbol and a strengthening of that abiding commitment to man's dignity and man's equality, which always has been the guiding purpose of the American Nation.

This law is the product, not of any man or group of men, but of a broad national consensus that every person is entitled to justice, to equality, and to a chance to enjoy the blessings of liberty. It is in the highest traditions of a civilization which from Magna Charta on has used the fabric of law for the fulfillment of liberty.

The Civil Rights Act is a challenge to men of good will to transform the commands of our law into the customs of our land. It is a challenge to all of us to go to work in our states, in our communities, in our homes, and, most of all, in the depths of our hearts, to eliminate the final strongholds of intolerance and hatred. It is a challenge to reach beyond the content of the bill, to conquer the barriers of poor education, poverty, squalid housing, which are legacies of past injustice and impediments to future advance. It sets goals to improve the lives of all underprivileged Americans.

We will achieve these goals because most Americans are law-abiding citizens who want to do what is right. That is why the Civil Rights Act relies first on voluntary compliance, then on the efforts of local communities and states to secure the rights of citizens. It provides for the national authority to step in only when others cannot or will not do the job.

Fulfillment of rights and prevention of disorder go hand in hand. Resort to violence blocks the path to racial justice. We must maintain law and order among our own citizens.

No person, whatever his grievance, can be allowed to attack the right of every American to be secure in his home, his shop, and in his streets. We will not permit any part of America to become a jungle, where the weak are the prey of the wanton.

Some of the reports which I read daily have given me cause for concern regarding organized violence by small groups who mask their identity. I condemn as do most Americans the use of violence and terror by clandestine hate organizations. Savagery of this or any other kind is alien to the entire moral and political tradition of the United States.

Such acts must be stopped and punished—whether they occur in Mississippi or in New York. Under our Constitution, the local authorities have the central responsibility for civil peace. There is no place in our Federal system for a national police force. But where help is needed or Federal law is violated, we shall be there. We will work together to punish all such lawbreakers, whether they be murderers in the countryside, or hooded nightriders on the highways, or hoodlums in the city.

Those who would hold back progress toward equality and, at the same time, promise racial peace, are deluding themselves and the people. Orderly progress and exact enforcement of law are the only path to an end of racial strife.

The time has come to cease telling ourselves and the world that the destiny of this Nation will be decided by street rioters and nightriders. The time has come to cease this cynical guessing about who will be helped and who will be hurt by disorders and disobedience and disrespect for the law. All will be hurt, none will be helped, if responsible citizens sit on the sidelines and regard the stability of our society as a spectator sport.

A problem older than any of us, older even than our Nation, as old as the history of man, has come upon us to test our system and to challenge our society. There are two courses open to us. We can meet the challenge, or we can turn away from it. We can master the problem, or we can leave it to master us.

Wherever we live, we must ask ourselves: Are we

prepared? Are we prepared to give up our prosperity and our peace and let our prejudices make paupers of us all? Are we of this generation to be remembered for allowing America's progress to run aground on the shoals of race prejudice? The answer must be, No. A nation of courage and compassion, a nation of common sense, must not allow its greatness to be degraded by those who work only for its division. The question before our Nation is not how whites will vote, or Negroes will vote, next November. The question is: How shall we work together and succeed together for the next hundred Novembers to come?

4

THE WAR ON POVERTY

"We have declared unconditional war on poverty.
Our objective is total victory."

I know what poverty means to people. I have been unemployed. I have stood in an employment office, waiting for an assignment and a placement. I have shined shoes as a boy. I have worked on a highway crew from daylight until dark for a dollar a day.

I remember the day the Bonus Army was driven down the streets to the mud flats of Anacostia. I remember as an NYA director back in the early days of the Roosevelt Administration when kids were riding the rails. We saw them getting their breakfast by culling grapefruit rinds that had been thrown in the garbage can.

. . .

I know the meaning of poverty. It means waiting in a surplus-food line rather than in a supermarket check-out. It means going without running water rather than worrying about whether you can afford a color television. It means despairing of finding work rather than wondering when you can take your vacation. It means coming home each night empty-handed to look at the expectant faces of your little children, who lack the things that they need. It means a lonely battle to maintain pride and self-respect in a family that you cannot provide for.

Poverty not only strikes at the needs of the body; it attacks the spirit and undermines human dignity.

There is a difference between being poor and being in poverty—a big difference. Many of us grew up poor. But while we were poor, we were not the prisoners of poverty; we were not caught in the backwash of an industrial revolution as the people of Appalachia are today. We had a chance to break out and to move up—a chance many Americans don't have.

Some people say that if Americans are poor, it is their own fault. I have even heard some argue that God ordains poverty for the poor. I don't believe them, and I don't think God believes them either.

I believe the reason most poor people are poor is that they never got a decent break.

Some people never got that break because they were born in the wrong part of the country; or because they were born with the wrong color of skin; or because they went into farming and couldn't get enough land to make a decent living when farm prices were too low and operating costs too high.

President Franklin D. Roosevelt once said that it is an unfortunate human failing that a full pocketbook often groans more loudly than an empty stomach. So long as I am President, I do not intend to allow the tempo of America's unprecedented prosperity to muffle the cries of those who are denied a fair share of it.

We have declared unconditional war on poverty. Our objective is total victory. Our soldiers in the cause can be men and women of both parties.

This war on poverty will enlist many recruits. First, almost half a million underprivileged young Americans will be given the opportunity to develop skills and continue their education and to find useful work. We are going to take care of our

41

children because one day our children will be taking care of America.

Second, every American community will have the opportunity to develop a comprehensive plan to fight its own poverty in its own way. We will help those communities carry out those plans. We are asking them to lead the way.

Third, dedicated Americans will have the opportunity to enlist as volunteers. I expect the women of America to be the first to enlist in this war for the benefit of their children—not only this generation, but the children of future generations. Two out of every five Peace Corps volunteers now serving overseas are women. At least two of every four volunteers in the war on poverty at home should be women.

It is not enough for the Congress to pass laws. We will not win our war against poverty until the conscience of the entire Nation is aroused. We will not succeed until every citizen regards the suffering of neighbors as a call to action.

I remember standing in front of the United States Capitol, as a young secretary to a Congressman, and watching Franklin Delano Roosevelt bravely grip the podium and declare, "The only thing we have to fear is fear itself." That moment gave me an inspiration which has lasted through the years.

In the angry bitterness of the Depression, we forged a vision for America. It is an America where every man has an equal chance for the well-being that is essential to the enjoyment of the freedom that we brag about. President Roosevelt talked of the one third of our nation who were ill clad and ill fed and ill housed. In thirty years of effort, we have brought that group down to one fifth. We still have a distance to go.

Head as well as heart tells us we must act. The poverty of other people is already a mounting burden. We are now paying $4 billion a year for public assistance. We are now paying $8 billion a year for police and health and fire departments. The costs are high and they are going higher. Unless we attack the causes of poverty, we are going to be shoveling funds to the tax consumers instead of making them taxpayers.

Waste is not unique to Washington. Sometimes greater waste comes from what a society leaves undone. Racial and religious discrimination last year, according to the President's Council of Economic Advisers, cost us $15 billion. Unused or underused manpower costs us even more. My Administration is dedicated to lifting off the burdens which weigh down our national productivity, our national expansion, and our national prosperity.

We must teach skills to those who have no skills. It costs money to do this. But if the nine million families who are poor can earn minimum incomes of $3,000 a year, personal income in the Nation will climb more than $11 billion per year.

We won the first American Revolution because we were a people in arms. We mobilized every resource of a new and weak country to defeat a great empire. Today America is richer and stronger. We have the resources and we have the knowledge to win this war on poverty.

The battle will not be spectacular. It will consist of thousands of small efforts that add up to a vast national effort. By small beginnings, we will move toward the goal that Franklin Roosevelt set before us when he called for a "more abundant life" for every man, woman, and child.

We are not trying to give people more relief— we want to give people more opportunity. That is what the people want. They want education and training. They want a job and a wage which will let them provide for their family. Above all, they want their children to escape the poverty which has afflicted them. They want, in short, to be part of a great nation, and that nation will never be great until all of the people are part of it.

5

TOWARD THE GREAT SOCIETY

"We have the opportunity to move, not only toward the rich society and the powerful society, but upward to the Great Society."

Franklin Delano Roosevelt once prophesied, "One day a generation may possess this land, blessed beyond anything we now know, blessed with those things—material and spiritual—that make man's life abundant. If that is the fashion of your dreaming then I say: 'Hold fast to your dream. America needs it.'"

Franklin D. Roosevelt and John F. Kennedy are gone. But our people still dream their dreams and we will carry on.

Old hopes have been reached and new horizons beckon us. This remains the land of the Great Experiment. The American story in the history of life on this planet is just beginning.

Forty years ago I left my high school diploma at home and headed west to seek the fame and fortune that I knew America offered. Almost two years later I came back to Johnson City, with empty hands and empty pockets. I came back because I realized that the place to begin was the place that I had been all the time.

Here, at this time, is the starting point of the path that leads to the future. Our society can be a place where we will raise our families, free from the dark shadow of war and suspicion among nations. It can be a place where our children will grow up knowing that success in life depends only on his ability and not on the color of his skin, or the creed of his religion, or the region of his birth. It can be a place where America is growing not only richer and stronger but happier and wiser. For whatever the strength of our arms, or whatever the size of our economy, we will not be a great nation unless we pursue excellence.

The purpose of protecting the life of our Nation and preserving the liberty of our citizens is to pursue the happiness of our people. Our success in that pursuit is the test of our success as a nation. For a century we labored to settle and to subdue a continent. For half a century we called upon unbounded invention and untiring industry to create an order of plenty for all of our people. The challenge of the next half century is whether we have the wisdom to use that wealth to enrich and elevate our national life, and to advance the quality of our American civilization.

Imagination, initiative, and indignation will determine whether we build a society where progress is the servant of our needs—or a society where old values and new visions are buried under unbridled growth. We have the opportunity to move, not only toward the rich society and the powerful society, but upward to the Great Society.

The Great Society rests on abundance and liberty for all. It demands an end to poverty and racial injustice. But that is just the beginning. The Great Society is a place where every child can find knowledge to enrich his mind and to enlarge his talents. It is a place where leisure is a welcome chance to build and reflect, not a feared cause of boredom and restlessness. It is a place where the city of man serves not only the needs of the body and the demands of commerce, but the desire for beauty and the hunger for community.

It is a place where man can renew contact with

nature. It is a place which honors creation for its own sake and for what it adds to the understanding of the race. It is a place where men are more concerned with the quality of their goals than the quantity of their goods. But most of all, the Great Society is not a safe harbor, a resting place, a final objective, a finished work. It is a challenge constantly renewed, beckoning us toward a destiny where the meaning of our lives matches the marvelous products of our labor.

There are three central places where we must begin to build the Great Society—in our cities, in our countryside, and in our classrooms.

Many living today will see the time, perhaps fifty years from now, when there will be four hundred million Americans, four fifths of them in urban areas. In the remainder of this century, urban population will double, city land will double, and we will have to build homes, highways, and facilities equal to all those built since this country was first settled. In the next forty years we must rebuild the entire urban United States.

Aristotle said, "Men come together in cities in order to live, but they remain together in order to live the good life."

. . .

It is harder and harder to live the good life in American cities today. The catalogue of ills is long. There is the decay of the centers and the despoiling of the suburbs. There is not enough housing for our people or transportation for our traffic. Open land is vanishing and old landmarks are violated. Worst of all, expansion is eroding the precious and time-honored values of community with neighbors and communion with nature. The loss of these values breeds loneliness and boredom and indifference.

Our society will never be great until our cities are great. Today the frontier of imagination and innovation is inside those cities and not beyond their borders. New experiments are already going on. It will be our task to make the American city a place where future generations will come, not only to live, but to live the good life.

A second place where we begin to build the Great Society is in our countryside. We have always prided ourselves on being not only America the strong and America the free but America the beautiful. Today that beauty is in danger. The water we drink, the food we eat, the very air that we breathe, are threatened with pollution. Our parks are overcrowded, our seashores overburdened. Green fields and dense forests are disappearing.

. . .

A few years ago we were greatly concerned about the Ugly American. Today we must act to prevent an Ugly America.

Once the battle is lost, once our natural splendor is destroyed, it can never be recaptured. And once man can no longer walk with beauty or wonder at nature, his spirit will wither and his sustenance be wasted.

A third place to build the Great Society is in the classrooms of America. There our children's lives will be shaped. Our society will not be great until every young mind is set free to scan the farthest reaches of thought and imagination.

We are still far from that goal. Today, eight million adult Americans have not finished five years of school. Nearly fifty-four million—more than one quarter of all America—have not even finished high school. Each year more than a hundred thousand high school graduates, with proven ability, do not enter college because they cannot afford it.

If we cannot educate today's youth, what will we do in 1970 when elementary school enrollment will be five million greater than in 1960? High school enrollment will rise by five million. College enrollment will increase by more than three million.

In many places, classrooms are overcrowded and curricula are outdated. Most of our qualified teachers are underpaid, and many of our paid teachers are unqualified. We must give every child a place to sit and a teacher to learn from. Poverty must not be a bar to learning, and learning must offer an escape from poverty.

But more classrooms and more teachers are not enough. We must seek an educational system which grows in quality as well as in size. This means better training for our teachers. It means preparing youth to enjoy their hours of leisure as well as their hours of labor. It means exploring new techniques of teaching, to find new ways to stimulate the love of learning and the capacity for creation.

These are three of the central issues of the Great Society. While our government has many programs directed at those issues, I do not pretend that we have the full answer to those problems. But I do promise this: We are going to assemble the best thought and the broadest knowledge from all over the world to find those answers for America.

We hear it said from time to time that the day of the individual is passing. We are told that this is the age of the oversized organization—of big business, of big unions, of big government. We hear that the individual is being smothered by giant concentrations of power. We are told that the individual can count for little in the era of The Organization Man.

Earlier generations also prophesied that the individual had reached his final frontier. Our ancestors complained bitterly when the West was won, leaving no new avenues of adventure or escape. At the turn of the century, prophets were predicting that men would be devoured by the monster corporation. During the dreary Depression years, some concluded that the future, if there were a future, belonged to the totalitarian society.

History has a habit of upsetting dire calculations. I believe that the pessimistic prophecies about our future are mistaken. We can shape a destiny in which the individual finds rich rewards.

This statement of faith is not based on an idle dream. As machines increasingly bring release from manual toil, I foresee little leisure for those who work with their minds. We have big problems ahead—and challenging times demand creative thinking.

- • •

Unless we stimulate individual enterprise, unless we regard individual accomplishment, we will be the servants and not the masters of change.

In education, we must provide higher learning for all who qualify. But we must also encourage the excellence which inspires a talented student to enlarge the limits of his capacity.

In science, achievement requires many technicians working in concert. But we must never forget the tradition of the solitary genius—the Newton, the Einstein, the Fermi—who tests the free range of his own curiosity.

In art, we welcome the growth of mass markets for books, painting, and sculpture. But we must also seek to nourish the artistic talent which has not yet achieved a buying public.

In the humanities, we must ensure that centers of liberal learning are not neglected as new knowledge nourishes the practical studies.

In all areas of public and private enterprise, we must understand that important ideas cannot be fashioned on an assembly line. The wit who told us that a camel was a horse designed by a committee deserves a medal.

We can and we must set priorities for individual accomplishment, and avoid mediocrity as the standard of success. These are wise and proper cautions to protect and promote individual expression in America.

At the same time, let us not call forth phantom fears about what the future holds. One of these fears often raised is that government has become a major menace to individual liberty. This is not so.

Does government subvert our freedom through the Social Security system which guards our people against destitution when they are too old to work? Does government undermine our freedom by bringing electricity to the farm, by controlling floods, or by ending bank failures? Is freedom lessened by efforts to abate pollution in our streams, by efforts to gain knowledge of the causes of heart disease and cancer, or by efforts to strengthen competition and the free market? Is freedom really diminished by banning the sale of harmful drugs, by providing school lunches for our children, by preserving our wilderness areas, or by improving the safety of our airways? Is freedom betrayed when in 1964 we redeem in full a pledge made a century ago by the Emancipation Proclamation?

The truth is—far from crushing the individual, government at its best liberates him from the enslaving forces of his environment. For, as Thomas Jefferson said, "The care of human life and happiness, and not their destruction, is the first and only legitimate object of good government."

A compassionate government keeps faith with the trust of the people and cherishes the future of their children. Through compassion for the plight of one individual, government fulfills its purpose as the servant of all the people.

Let me state clearly what I mean by "government." I do not mean just the politicians, technicians, and experts in Washington. I do not mean only the agencies that make up the Federal system, or the departments and bureaus of state government or local municipalities. I include every citizen. For as Aristotle said, "If liberty and equality . . . are chiefly to be found in democracy, they will be best attained when all persons alike share in the government to the utmost."

We have in this country a government which derives its power from the consent of the governed —from the people. From those same people must come the dreams, the faith, the hopes, and the works which fashion the great purpose of government. From the people must come the private compassion and the personal commitment by which struggles for justice and wars against poverty are won.

. . .

Because our government is the sum total of the people it serves, the choices that we personally make, the courses that we personally follow, the contests that we personally join—these will finally decide the real character of this country.

I do not doubt history's verdict. I believe that thirty years from now Americans will look back upon these 1960s as the time of the great American Breakthrough—toward the victory of peace over war; toward the victory of prosperity over poverty; toward the victory of human rights over human wrongs; toward the victory of enlightened minds over darkness.

6

THE NATURE OF THE COMMUNIST THREAT

"Communists, using force and intrigue, seek to bring about a communist-dominated world. Our convictions, our interests, our life as a nation demand that we resolutely oppose, with all of our might, that effort to dominate the world."

We live at a time when foreign affairs go beyond their traditional scope; they now have strong new ties with the domestic life of every country.

These new ties come

—from modern communications, which bring instantly to the homes of citizens in every country the news of events from round the world;

—from modern weapons, which make the threat of war anywhere a life-and-death issue for every nation;

• • •

—from the fact that we are all involved in historic changes, which are reshaping the political life of the planet.

I have in mind the change from the colonial era to an era when scores of new nations claim rights and recognition; the change from old to modern societies, which can bring to their peoples the advantages of modern science and technology; the change in Western Europe, Japan, and elsewhere from postwar dependence upon the United States to partnership in the affairs of the planet; and the change, we hope, from dangerous cold war to a more stable and peaceful world.

None of these changes is automatic. All will take time. All can be upset. All can bring threats to the peace. None will succeed if we do not accept the fact of the world's interdependence.

Since the end of World War II, America has been found wherever freedom was under attack or wherever world peace was threatened. The stage has shifted many times. The stakes have grown as man's capacity for destruction grew. But America's role has not changed. With constancy we have pursued the defense of freedom and we have prevented nuclear destruction. We have patiently labored to construct a world order in which both peace and freedom could flourish.

We have lived so long with crisis and danger that we accept, almost without discussion, the assumption of American concern for disorders that threaten the peace in other parts of the world. Yet this is a unique responsibility—unique for America and unique in history. First, we accepted this responsibility because at one time no other nation could do it. For the last twenty years, only under the shadow of our strength could friends keep their freedom. Second, we have learned, at painful cost, that we can no longer wait for the tides of conflict to touch our shores. Aggression and upheaval, in any part of the world, carry the seeds of destruction to our own freedom and to civilization itself.

Finally, we have a reason that is often difficult for others to understand. We have accepted responsibility because it is right that we should. Cynics often underestimate the strong thread of moral purpose which runs through the fabric of American history. Of course, our policies are shaped with a proper regard for our security and welfare. But much of the energy of our efforts has come from this moral purpose.

We know it is right that the strong should help the weak defend their freedom; that the wealthy should help the poor emerge from their hunger;

that nations should be free from the coercion of others.

There is another value which guides America's course. It is the deep American belief in the peaceful process of orderly settlement. We regard it as our duty to help settle any conflict which might erupt into a wider arena. It is our duty to work toward the acceptance of the principle that disputes should be settled without force—among allies and enemies alike.

Communists, using force and intrigue, seek to bring about a communist-dominated world. Our convictions, our interests, our life as a nation demand that we resolutely oppose, with all of our might, that effort to dominate the world.

The Gulf of Tonkin may be distant Asian waters, but none can be detached about what happened there. Aggression—deliberate, willful, and systematic aggression—unmasked its face to the entire world. The world remembers—the world must never forget—that aggression unchallenged is aggression unleashed.

We of the United States have not forgotten. That is why we answered this aggression with action.

America's course was not precipitate. America's response was not without long provocation. For ten years Presidents Eisenhower and Kennedy, and I have been actively concerned with threats to the peace and security of the peoples of Southeast Asia from the communist government of North Vietnam.

President Eisenhower sought, and President Kennedy sought, the same objectives that I still seek: That the governments of Southeast Asia honor the international agreements which apply in the area; that those governments leave each other alone; that they resolve their differences peacefully; that they devote their talents to bettering the lives of their peoples by working against poverty and disease and ignorance.

Some say that we should withdraw from South Vietnam, and come home. But the United States cannot and will not turn aside and allow the freedom of a brave people to be handed over to communist tyranny. This alternative is strategically unwise and it is morally unthinkable.

Others are eager to enlarge the conflict. They call upon us to supply American boys to do the job that Asian boys should do. They ask us to take reckless action which would risk the lives of millions, engulf much of Asia, and threaten the peace

67

of the entire world. Such action would offer no solution to the real problem of Vietnam.

America can and America will meet any wider challenge from others. But our aim in Vietnam, as in the rest of the world, is to help restore the peace and to re-establish a decent order.

Wherever the forces of freedom are engaged, no one who commands the power of nuclear weapons can escape his responsibility for the life of our people. We do not intend to place this Nation in danger by threatening nuclear war at each and every provocation. No American President has ever pursued so irresponsible a course. Our firmness at moments of crisis has always been matched by restraint, our determination by care. It was so under President Truman in Berlin, under President Eisenhower in the Formosa Straits, under President Kennedy in the Cuba missile crisis—and it will be so as long as I am President.

The course that we have chosen requires wisdom and endurance. No one should doubt for a moment that we have the resources and the will to follow this course as long as it may take. No one should think that we will be worn down, nor will we be driven out. We will not be provoked into rashness;

but we will continue to meet aggression with firmness, and unprovoked attack with measured reply.

The challenge that we face in Southeast Asia is the same challenge that we have faced with courage and that we have met with strength in Greece and Turkey, in Berlin and Korea, in Lebanon and in Cuba.

I would like to make clear to ally and to adversary alike: Let no friend needlessly fear—and no foe vainly hope—that this is a nation divided in this election year. Our free elections are America's strength, not America's weakness.

7

THE NECESSITY
FOR STRENGTH

"There is no place in today's world for weakness. But there is also no place in today's world for recklessness."

All my life we have been either preparing for war or fighting a war or protecting ourselves from war. When I was a child, one of my first memories was hearing the powder go off on an anvil on Armistice Day. I remember the terror that flowed from the *Lusitania*. I remember seeing boys come marching home, and the welcome we gave them at our little schoolhouse. When Pearl Harbor was attacked, I remember leaving, the day after I voted, to go to the South Pacific, and later to the Atlantic. I have witnessed the billions and billions of dollars we have spent in the nineteen years since that war, to protect Western civilization.

Today we share responsibility not only for our

own security but for the security of all free nations. Such responsibility requires more than national strength. It requires, first of all, a nation dedicated to justice and to the improvement of life for its own people. It requires a nation determined to help others eliminate the despair and the human degradation on which the enemies of freedom feed. It requires a nation devoted, through speech and deed, to showing those who may grow weary of will, or fearful of the future, that the cause of human dignity is on the march.

But our hope for success in the aims of peace rests also on the strength of our arms. As Winston Churchill once said: "Civilization will not last, freedom will not survive, peace will not be kept, unless a very large majority of mankind unite together to defend them and show themselves possessed of a constabulary power before which barbaric and atavistic forces will stand in awe."

We, as well as our adversaries, must stand in awe before the power our craft has created. In every area, America today is stronger than she has ever been before. She is stronger than any adversary or combination of adversaries. She is stronger than the combined might of all the nations in the history of the world. And that strength is increasing.

The first area of this increasing strength is our ability to deter atomic destruction. Since January, 1961, we have increased our nuclear power on alert two and one half times. We have more than a thousand fully armed ICBMs and Polaris missiles ready for retaliation. The Soviet Union has far fewer, and none equivalent to our Polaris. We have eleven hundred strategic bombers, including over five hundred on fifteen-minute alert. Many of these bombers are equipped with air-to-surface and decoy missiles to help them reach almost any target.

Against such force the combined destructive power of every battle ever fought by man is like a firecracker thrown against the sun.

The second area of increasing strength is our ability to fight less than all-out war. In the past three and a half years we have raised the number of combat-ready Army divisions 45 per cent. They can be moved swiftly around the world by an airlift capacity which has increased 75 per cent. Supporting tactical aircraft have been increased by 44 per cent, and the number of tactical nuclear warheads in Continental Europe has been raised 60 per cent. We and our NATO allies now have five million men under arms. In addition we are now ready to mobilize large reserves in the event of conflict. Six divisions, with all supporting units, can be moved into action in a few weeks.

• • •

A third area of increasing strength is the struggle against subversion. Our adversaries, convinced that direct attack would be aimless, today resort to terrorism and guerrilla warfare. To meet this threat we began a large effort to train special forces to fight internal subversion. We have increased our specialized forces eight times. We have trained more than a hundred thousand officers in guerrilla techniques. We have given special emphasis to this form of warfare in the training of all military units.

Our Army now has six Special Action Forces on call around the world to assist friendly nations, skilled in the languages and problems of the area in which they are stationed. The Navy and Air Force have several thousand men whose abilities, training, equipment, and mission are designed to combat clandestine attack. And behind these groups are five brigade-size backup forces ready to move into instant action.

Just as subversion has many faces, our responses must take many forms. We have worked to increase and integrate all the resources, political and social as well as military and economic, needed to meet a threat which tears at the entire fabric of a society.

But success in fighting subversion rests ultimately

on the skill of the soldiers of the threatened country. We now have 344 teams at work in 49 countries to train the local military in the most advanced techniques of internal defense. Such conflict requires weapons as well as will. We will continue to increase this strength until our adversaries are convinced that this course will not lead to conquest.

The fourth area of increasing strength is in the development of new weapons for deterrence and defense. In the past several years we have begun many important new weapons systems. Minuteman II will have twice the accuracy of the first Minuteman. The new Nike-X, when its development is completed, will give us the option to deploy the best anti-ballistics missile available to any nation. We are developing a new aircraft, the F-111, with much greater range, payload, and ability in air combat than present tactical bombers or fighters.

The LANCE Missile, the EX-10 torpedo, the A7A attack aircraft, a new battle tank, and new antitank missile systems are the emerging products of development that we are carrying on. I can assure the American people that the United States is and will remain first in the use of science and technology for the protection of the people.

The fifth area of increasing strength is the ability of the American fighting man. Our weapons can be no better than the men who employ them. The complexities of modern weapons require soldiers of high skill. The complexities of modern warfare require men of knowledge. The complexities of the modern world require men of broad outlook. Our training programs have been expanded to provide this greater wisdom.

The necessities of our strength are as varied as the nature of our dangers. The response must suit the threat. Those who would answer every problem with nuclear weapons display not bravery but bravado, not wisdom but a wanton disregard for the survival of the world and the future of the race.

No one can live daily with the dark realities of nuclear ruin without seeking the guidance of God to find the path of peace. We have built this staggering strength, not to destroy but to save, not to put an end to civilization but to try to put an end to conflict.

There is no place in today's world for weakness. But there is also no place in today's world for recklessness. We cannot act rashly with the nuclear weapons that could destroy us all. The only course is to press with all our mind and all our will to make sure, doubly sure, that these weapons are never used.

8

BUILDING THE
ATLANTIC PARTNERSHIP

"I predict that the years to come will see us draw
closer to General Marshall's bold design than at
any time since he stood at Harvard and began to
reshape the world."

Fifteen years ago, here in Washington, the North Atlantic Treaty was signed. Less than five months later, after due constitutional process in all the signing countries, the Treaty entered into force. From that time to this, the Treaty has served the peace of the world.

This short Treaty commits its parties to consider an armed attack on any of them in Europe or North America as "an attack against them all." For fifteen years it has prevented any such attack. Created in response to Stalin's Iron Curtain and the loss of Czechoslovakian freedom, this Treaty has lived through war in Korea, the threat of war over

Berlin, and a crisis without precedent in Cuba. Each great event has tested NATO, and from each test we have gained increased strength.

What began as a Treaty soon became a Command and then a great international organization. The number of ready M-Day divisions in Europe has increased fourfold. The number of modern aircraft has multiplied by ten—all more effective by far than any were in 1949.

The alliance is real. Its forces operate. Its strength is known. Its weapons cover the full range of power, from small arms to nuclear missiles of the most modern design.

From the beginning our Atlantic partnership has aimed not simply at defense, but at the cooperative progress of all its members. President Truman described the Treaty as a "bulwark which will permit us to get on with the real business of government and society, the business of achieving a fuller and happier life for all of our citizens." It came, in fact, two years after we and other friends had begun our joint enterprise for economic recovery under the Marshall Plan.

The years since then have seen the longest surge of economic growth that our Atlantic world has ever known. Our production and trade have more than doubled; our population has grown by more than a hundred million; the income of the average man has grown by more than 50 per cent. Our inward peace and our outward confidence have grown steadily more secure. The internal threat of communism has shriveled with repeated failure.

Danger has receded, but it has not disappeared. The task of building our defenses is never really done. The temptation to relax must always be resisted. Our common task is to move onward to that closer partnership which is so plainly in our common interest.

The United States, for one, has learned much from fifteen years of danger and achievement. In 1949 the solemn commitment of this Treaty was for us an historic departure from isolation. Now it is a tested and recognized foundation stone of America's foreign policy. What Robert Schuman said for France in 1949 I repeat for my country: "Nations are more and more convinced that their fates are closely bound together; their salvation and their welfare can no longer be based upon an egotistical and aggressive nationalism, but must rest upon the progressive application of human solidarity."

The ways of our growing partnership are not easy. Though the union of Europe is her manifest destiny, the building of that unity is a long, hard job. But we, for our part, will never turn back to separated insecurity. We welcome the new strength of our transatlantic allies. We find no contradiction between national self-respect and interdependent mutual reliance. We are eager to share with the new Europe at every level of power and responsibility. We aim to share the lead in the search for new and stronger patterns of co-operation.

The Atlantic peoples have a magnificent history, but they have known too much war. It is the splendor of this great alliance that in keeping peace with its opponents it has kept the road clear for a worldwide march toward the good life for free people.

To General Marshall and those who shared in shaping his plan, permanent peace depended upon rebuilding all European civilization within its historic boundaries. The Iron Curtain rang down upon that vision. But its correctness has not changed. It will not be achieved by sudden settlement or by dramatic deed. But the nations of Eastern Europe are beginning to reassert their own identity. There is no longer a single Iron Curtain. There are many. Each differs in strength and thickness—in the light that can pass through it and the hopes that can prosper behind it.

We do not know when all European nations will

become part of a single civilization. But as President Eisenhower said in 1953: "This we do know: a world that begins to witness the rebirth of trust among nations can find its way to a peace that is neither partial nor punitive."

We will continue to build bridges across the gulf which has divided us from Eastern Europe—bridges of trade, of ideas, of visitors, and of humanitarian aid. We do this for four reasons: First, to open new relationships to countries seeking increased independence yet unable to risk isolation. Second, to open the minds of a new generation to the values and the visions of the Western civilization from which they come and to which they belong. Third, to give play to the powerful forces of national pride as the strongest barrier against the ambition of any country to dominate another. Fourth, to demonstrate that prospects of progress for Eastern Europe lie in a wider relationship with the West.

We go forward within the framework of our unalterable commitment to the defense of Europe and to the reunification of Germany. But America and Western Europe have achieved the strength and self-confidence to follow a course based on hope rather than hostility, based on opportunity rather than fear. It is our belief that wise and skillful development of relationships with the nations of Eastern Europe can speed the day when Germany will be reunited.

We are pledged to use every peaceful means to work with friends and allies so that all of Europe may be joined in a shared society of freedom. I predict that the years to come will see us draw closer to General Marshall's bold design than at any time since he stood at Harvard and began to reshape the world.

9

THIS DEVELOPING WORLD

"The world cannot remain divided between rich nations and poor nations, or white nations and colored nations. In such division are the seeds of terrible discord and danger in decades to come. For the wall between rich and poor is a wall of glass through which all can see."

Within six months of each other, two of the great men of this century passed from this earth: President John F. Kennedy and Pope John XXIII. Both left a world transformed. Both handed on a vision of the future which will occupy the thoughts and labors of men during years ahead.

For a generation, Americans have struggled to keep the ambitions of nations from erupting into the annihilation of nuclear war. We have struggled to diminish hostility and to decrease tension, while battling aggression and building our power. But even if we achieve such a world, we will only have taken a first step toward final fulfillment of the hopes of Pope John and President Kennedy. For just as the cold war has consumed our energies, it has often limited our horizons. We have tended to place every challenge in the context of conflict, to regard every difficulty as part of a struggle for domination.

Even if we end terror and even if we eliminate tension, even if we reduce arms and restrict conflict, even if peace were to come to the nations, we would turn from this struggle only to find ourselves on a new battleground as filled with danger and as fraught with difficulty as any ever faced by man. For many of our most urgent problems do not spring from the cold war or even from the ambitions of our adversaries.

These are the problems which will persist beyond the cold war. They are the obstacles to man's effort to build a great world society—a place where every man can find a life free from hunger and disease, a life offering the chance to seek spiritual fulfillment unhampered by the degradation of bodily misery.

These long years of conflict have given fresh content to the old observation that no man, and no community, and no nation, is an island. This truth, borne in upon us by the necessities of our protection, is equally true for those problems which stretch beyond present differences. Those who live in the emerging community of nations will ignore the problems of their neighbors at their own peril.

It may seem difficult to accept the fact that even lasting peace will not contain respite from world responsibility. But we must learn to bring to the challenges which lie beyond the present conflict the same qualities of resolution and compassion that we have brought to the protection of freedom.

Three problems, among others, menace man's welfare and will threaten it even when armed destruction and war are things of the past. They are the problems of poverty, of disease, and of diminishing natural resources.

First is the problem of poverty—the separation between the rich and poor nations. Today the per capita product of the developed countries is $1,730 a year. In the developing countries it is $143. And the gap is widening, not narrowing. Our own growth must continue. But we must find ways to step up the growth of others or we will be an increasingly isolated island of wealth in the midst of mounting misery.

Second is man's struggle against disease, the focal point in his war to control the destructive forces of nature. Each year three million people die from tuberculosis. Each year five million die from dysentery, half a million from measles. In some countries, one sixth of the entire population suffers from leprosy. Yet we have the knowledge to reduce the toll of these diseases.

Third is the need to develop new resources and new ways to use existing resources. It has been estimated that if everyone in the world were to rise to the level of living of those in the United States, we would then have to extract about 20 billion tons of iron, 300 million tons of copper, 300 million tons of lead, and 200 million tons of zinc. These totals are well over a hundred times the world's present annual rate of production.

There is no simple solution to these problems. In the past there would have been no solution at all. Today the constantly unfolding conquests of science give man a power over his world which can bring the prospect of success within the purview of hope.

On three continents, in dozens of countries, hundreds of millions of people struggle to exist on incomes of little more than a dollar a week. Many people have less to spend each day on food and on shelter and clothing, on medicine, on all of their needs, than the average American spends at his corner drug store for a package of cigarettes. They live in rundown country shacks of tar paper. They live in city slums. They live without heat, water, sanitation, or hope.

Their children have no schools. They have no doctors or hospitals. Their life expectancy is between thirty-five and forty years of age. They see no escape from the ancient cycle of misery and despair.

These are not new conditions. Poverty, hunger, and disease are afflictions as old as man himself. But in our time and in this age there has been a change. The change is not so much in the realities of life, but in the hopes and the expectations for the future. If a peaceful revolution is impossible, a violent revolution is inevitable.

The shrinking of distances and the ready access to information has made us more aware of other people. It has also made them aware that a better life may be within their grasp. They know that the conditions that their fathers accepted with weary resignation are no longer inevitable. They know that depression and despair are not the ordained lot of man.

This knowledge has helped create the worldwide unrest which we describe as the revolution of rising expectations. The meaning of this revolution is very simple: It means that people in the rest of the world want for themselves the same things that you and I want for our loved ones, for our friends, and for our children. They want their families to live decent lives and have jobs that give them survival and dignity. They want their children to be taught to read and to write. They want the hungry to be fed and the sick to be treated. They intend to take their place in the great movement of modern society, to share in the benefits of that society.

These just desires have been unleashed. The people of the developing world are on the march, and we want to be beside them on that march. Our Gross National Product in this richest of all nations is running at an annual rate of over $618 billion. We are distributing in the form of aid and military assistance about one half of one per cent of that amount. This investment is not only one of the most noble acts that a great country could perform, but it is an act of necessity if we are to preserve our leadership in the world.

We must help developing countries because our own welfare demands it. It takes no great gift of foresight to realize that unless there is progress, there will be discontent. The developing world would soon become a cauldron of violence and hatred. Communism, with its false and easy promises of a magic formula, would find widespread and ready-made conditions for revolution. Every American who is concerned about the future of his country must also be concerned about the future of Africa, Asia, and our old friends in Latin America.

A great Central American patriot once said, "To have rights but live in rags is bitter living." The Alliance for Progress is transforming the bitter living of the underprivileged in Latin America. It seeks to show that democracy is more than voting. It is also living. We are working together to achieve economic progress, social justice, and, as the author of our Declaration of Independence said, to oppose "every form of tyranny over the mind of man."

The Charter of the Alliance charges each American country to seek and to strengthen representative democracy. Without that democracy and without the freedom that it nourishes, material progress is an aimless enterprise, destroying the dignity of the spirit that it is meant to liberate. So we will continue to encourage democracy until we build a hemisphere of free nations from the Tierra del Fuego to the Arctic Circle.

But the Charter is not confined to political democracy. It commands a peaceful, democratic, social revolution across the Hemisphere. It calls upon us to throw open the gates of opportunity to the landless and the despised. It asks that unjust privilege be ended and that unfair power be curbed.

The use of Cuba as a base for subversion and terror is an obstacle to our hopes for the Western Hemisphere. Our first task must be, as it has been, to isolate Cuba from the Inter-American system, to frustrate her efforts to destroy free governments, and to expose the weakness of communism so that all can see. That policy is working. The problems of this Hemisphere would be far more serious if Castro today sat at the councils of the Organization of American States, disrupting debates and blocking decision, if Castro had open channels of trade and communication along which subversion and terror could flow, if his economy had been a successful model rather than a dismal warning to all of his neighbors.

We will join with those throughout the Hemisphere who seek to advance their own democratic revolution. We recognize that it is not easy to change the customs of centuries. Some seek to halt reform and change. Others seek to impose terror and tyranny. But Bolivar's wisdom is our warning: "To hesitate is destruction."

The President and his family

President Johnson addressing a joint session of Congress

The President presides over the National Security Council

The President attends the Boy Scout Jamboree

The President meets the Press

Breakfast with the legislative leaders

The President visits Appalachia

The President confers with a North Carolina constituent

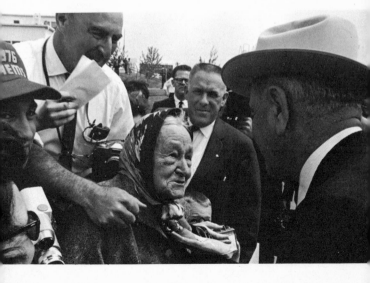

President Johnson signs the Higher Education Bill

The Ambassador from Kenya presents his credentials

The President and the First Lady hold a formal reception for
Chancellor Ludwig Erhard of Germany

Secretary General U Thant welcomes President Johnson during visit to the United Nations

No President who looks beyond the immediate problems which crowd his desk can fail to extend the hand and heart of this country to those who are struggling elsewhere. We help others in many ways, through trade and raw materials and manufactures, through the Peace Corps that has carried American idealism and know-how to almost fifty nations, through our Food for Peace, and through the exchange of scholars and students and ideas.

We know that we have much to gain from this exchange. We know that we can learn from the culture, the arts, and the traditions of other countries. Many of them are as rich in spiritual treasure as they are poor in material goods.

People everywhere are as hungry for respect as they are hungry for bread. There are societies in other lands now venturing to take the same step that our Colonial forefathers took when they brought into existence this, the most powerful of all nations.

America's great strength in world affairs is not in Washington alone. It rests on dedicated labor of our private institutions. It rests on organizations and local governments. It rests on the leaders and molders of public opinion. If we can summon all our strengths to promote our relations with the developing world, then we will have a weapon which our adversaries cannot hope to match. Then all

Americans will be proudly joined in a great adventure which unites the highest of our national ideals and the most important of our national needs.

The world cannot remain divided between rich nations and poor nations, or white nations and colored nations. In such division are the seeds of terrible discord and danger in decades to come. For the wall between rich and poor is a wall of glass through which all can see.

10

THE QUEST FOR PEACE

". . . as long as I am President, I will spare neither
my office nor myself in the quest for peace."

The Bible counsels us: "To every thing there is a season, and a time to every purpose under the heaven . . . a time of war and a time of peace."

After decades of war and threats of war, we may be nearing a time of peace. Today, as always, if a nation is to keep its freedom it must be prepared to risk war. When necessary, we will take that risk. But as long as I am President, I will spare neither my office nor myself in the quest for peace. That peace is much more than the absence of war. In fact, peace is much the same thing in our world community as it is in the small community of Johnson City, Texas, where I grew up.

.   .   .

If every morning brings fear that the serenity of the streets will be shattered by the sounds of violence, then there is no peace. If one man can compel others, unjustly and unlawfully, to do what he commands them to do, then a community is not a place of peace. If we have neither the will nor the way to settle disputes among neighbors without violence, then none of us can live in peace. If we do not work together to help others fulfill their just desires, then peace is insecure.

In a community, as in the world, if the strong and the wealthy ignore the needs of the poor and the oppressed, frustrations will lead to force. Peace, therefore, is a world where no nation fears another, and no nation can force another to follow its command. It is a world where differences are solved without destruction, and common effort is directed at common problems.

Such a peace will not come by a single act or in a single moment. It will take decades and generations of persistent and patient effort. That great son of Sweden, Dag Hammarskjöld, once said of peace: "The qualities it requires are just those which I feel we all need today: perseverance and patience, a firm grip on realities, careful but imaginative planning, a clear awareness of the dangers but also of the fact that fate is what we make it. . . ."

With these qualities as our foundation, we follow several paths toward the single goal of peace. What are those paths? First is the path of restraint in the use of power. We must be, and we are, strong enough to protect ourselves and our allies. But it was a great historian who reminded us: "No aspect of power more impresses men than its exercise with restraint."

We do not advance the cause of freedom by calling on the full might of our military to solve every problem. We won a great victory in Cuba, because we stood, for many days, firm without using force. In Vietnam we are engaged in a brutal and a bitter struggle, trying to help our friends. There, too, we will stand firm to help maintain their freedom, giving them advice and aid as necessary.

A second path is the search for practical solutions to particular problems. Agreements will not flow from a sudden trust among nations. Trust comes from a long series of agreements. Each agreement must be fashioned with attention to detail, with skill, with faith in the importance of the result.

And so, even while we are caught in conflict in one part of the world, we labor to build the structure of agreement which can bring peace to the rest of the world. We have signed a treaty ending nuclear tests in the atmosphere. We have cut back our production of atomic fuel and weapons. We have established a hot line between Washington and Moscow. We are meeting with the Soviets to pool our knowledge about making fresh water from the oceans. These agreements, by themselves, have not ended tensions; they have not ended the risks of war. But because of them we have moved closer to peace.

A third path lies in showing proper respect for the rights and fears of others. We can never compromise the cause of freedom. But as we work in our world community we must always remember that differences with others can come from honest clash of honest beliefs. Our strength does not entitle us to impose our interest. Rather, our desire for peace compels us to seek just agreements.

Other nations may honestly fear our intentions or the intentions of our allies. Where such fear exists, we must work to dispel that fear.

A fourth path toward peace must be followed by co-operating to solve the problems which are greater than immediate conflicts. Most of our neighbors in the world live in the midst of hunger and poverty. Most of our neighbors live in the midst of disease and ignorance. We are proud of the fact that throughout the world American workers and food and capital are building industry, expanding farms, educating the young, caring for the sick, and feeding the hungry.

A fifth path lies in adjusting disputes without the use of force. It is, in short, the pursuit of justice. We can find guidance here in our own country's historic pledge to the rule of law. It is a pledge to respect, uphold, and always obey the law of the land. For if any take grievances and disputes into their own hands, the safety and the freedom of all are in peril.

"Due process" is the safeguard of our civilization. The key to peace in our own land is obedience to the great moral command that no man should deny to another his rights under the Constitution. And it rests on the even more hallowed rule that whatever our disagreements, we treat others with peaceful respect. So, too, we seek a world community in which answers can win acceptance without the use of force. All the machinery of international justice is useless unless it is infused with the good faith of nations.

On a world-wide basis, we place much hope in the United Nations. Like all human institutions, the United Nations has not fulfilled the hopes that some held at its birth. Our understanding of how to live with one another is still far behind our knowledge of how to destroy one another. But as our problems have grown, this organization has grown, in membership, in authority, in prestige, in responsibility, and in maturity.

We have seen too much success to become obsessed with failure. The peace-keeping machinery of the United Nations has worked in the Far East, in the Western Pacific, in the Middle East, in Africa and the Mediterranean—forestalling or containing a dozen conflicts which might have spread into global war. The great transition from colonial rule to independence has been largely accomplished. The Decade of Development has successfully begun. The world arms race has been slowed. The struggle for human rights has been gaining new force.

A start has been made in furthering mankind's common interest in outer space, in scientific exploration, in communications, in weather forecasting, in banning the stationing of nuclear weapons, and in establishing principles of law.

I know that vast problems remain—conflicts between the great powers, conflicts between small neighbors, disagreements over disarmament, persistence of ancient wrongs in the area of human rights, residual problems of colonialism, and all the rest. Men and nations working apart created these problems; men and nations working together must solve them.

They can solve them when all members make the United Nations a workshop for constructive action, and not a forum for abuse; when all members seek UN help in settling their own disputes as well as the disputes of others; when all members meet their financial obligations to it; and when all members recognize that no nation and no party and no single system can control the future of man.

Agreement on control and reduction of weapons is not as impossible as it seemed for so many years. We have taken steps in the right direction. Now we must go further. Just as we are determined to do whatever must be done to defend our freedom and to deter aggression, so must we be equally determined to reduce the risks of another world-wide war.

If we have the genius to create these terrible weapons of destruction, then, certainly, we have the genius to create the means of their control. There will be doubts and delays and disappointments, but the pursuit of peace must continue. The United States is asking the world to take further steps toward peace, enforceable steps which can endanger no one's safety and will enlarge everyone's security.

I face a choice which only two other Presidents of the United States have confronted—whether our civilization, as we know it, will survive. For nuclear catastrophe is no longer merely a theoretical possibility. Today there are a dozen combustion points in the world. Tomorrow there may be more. We must deal with these disturbances.

But the world has changed and so has the method of dealing with disruptions of the peace. There may have been a time when a Commander-in-Chief would order soldiers to march the very moment a disturbance occurred. Once upon a time large-scale war could be waged without risking the end of civilization; today, such war is unthinkable. In a matter of moments, we could wipe out a hundred million of our adversaries. They could, in the same amount of time, wipe out a hundred million of our people, taking half of our land in a matter of an hour.

The people of the world prefer reasoned agreement to ready attack. That is why we must follow the Prophet Isaiah, saying, "Come now, let us reason together."

We envy no neighbor. We covet no territory. We

are looking for no satellites. We believe the most plausible solution to war is simply for each nation to leave its neighbors in peace. This would free us all to attack those ancient enemies of all mankind that for centuries have warred on man and his hope—poverty and ignorance, misery and disease. If we will join together to destroy them, we will destroy the roots of war.

11

OUR FREE SYSTEM

Capitalism in the United States today is not the capitalism known anywhere at any time in the past. The angry slogans of communism are archaic when directed against the capitalism of the American people. Under our system the worker is also the investor. The people are also the owners.

Capitalism in America is what it is today because of the initiative, the enterprise, and the responsibility of our free system. But it is also what it is because of the course that we have chosen for this government to follow.

•   •   •

We rejected the idea that the role of government is either coercion or control. On the contrary, the proper function of government is to conduct itself so that the people may have confidence in their future, in their system, and in themselves.

I believe we have created that confidence. For the past three and a half years we have had the longest and largest peacetime expansion of our economy on record. These years from 1961 through 1964 are going into the record books as the most prosperous of our history. It is prosperity not just for business-men—but for all the people.

Over 72 million Americans are at work—a new high. Gross National Product is up $117 billion—to a total of $618 billion. Industrial production is up 28.5 per cent. Stocks are worth $175 billion more.

But there is more. Profits and jobs are going hand in hand. Workers are gaining in purchasing power through fuller employment, longer hours, and higher wages. Higher wages have not increased the cost of doing business because productivity has risen to match the wages. Both business and labor are making their economic gains by enlarging the size of the economic pie. They are not making gains by taking bigger slices at the expense of one another or at the expense of the American consumer.

•   •   •

Our prosperity today is not a fleeting phenomenon. It is a solid, stable, steady prosperity—achieved by the confidence and certainty of a climate free of doubt and division and bitter contention. Our dollar is strong because the world has new confidence in our responsibility. Our consumer market is strong because Americans at home have confidence in our future course.

One reason our enterprise system is functioning successfully is that we have been doing in Washington many of the things so long needed to lift off burdens of the past. Government seeks to be not a dictator but a moderator, not a master planner but a faithful public servant, not an agent for control but an agent for freedom.

What we have accomplished can be lost if we do not continue on a wise course. We are in the midst of a growing revolution in our patterns of work. Technology is eliminating jobs for some and requiring higher skills from others. Our labor force is getting younger as our population grows and more women are returning to work. It is a primary responsibility to match the changing needs of business and the changing requirements of workers.

Our free enterprise system has met and surmounted the grave challenges of the past. Our ability to meet new challenges in the midst of a rapidly changing technology and a rapidly growing population is a test of America's future vision and vitality.

12

CREATIVE FEDERALISM

There has been much loose talk about the Federal Government versus the states' governments— as if they were enemies of one another. The American system is the fortunate one of Federalism. James Madison called it the happy combination. The Founding Fathers in their wisdom set up both state and national governments.

Their purpose was for each to do what it could do best. The Federal Government was not, as some would have it, an alien invention.

Both the Federal and state governments have always exercised leadership in solving the problems of the Nation. They are not, they must not be, rivals for the citizen's loyalty. They are separate agencies, each wtih special resources, each with special capabilities, but both joined in a united attack on the common problems of our country.

At times one or another has not pulled its full weight. Early in the twentieth century the Federal Government was doing far too little to protect and to advance the welfare of the general public. When we look back, we wonder how we avoided more serious revolt against its inactivity.

Today we are clearly moving into another era of our Federal system—an era of revitalization of our states. A fresh generation of energetic governors and reactivated legislatures is on the move. They are thinking and acting to meet their peoples' needs. One statistic suggests the whole trend. From 1952 to 1963, Federal expenditures have increased by less than one third. State and local expenditures have more than doubled.

The best government is the one closest to the people but also one which can accomplish its proper tasks. I would not want my county commissioner to recommend the plan for the Gulf of Tonkin. But I would not want the Chairman of my

Joint Chiefs of Staff to grade the road that leads to my schoolhouse.

That is why I am intensely interested in efforts to determine who can best do the job. This is democracy functioning in its most effective way—citizens calling on their own experts from their own communities to solve their own problems.

We must encourage such efforts. The White House has not the slightest interest in directing such efforts. We live by the belief that our Federal Government exists not to grow larger itself, but to encourage the people to grow larger than any or all of their governments. The Federal Government does not exist to subordinate the sovereign states. We exist to support them. As long as I am here, we are going to work and to co-operate with them.

There is one point that we must always bear in mind. It is that government by checks and balances will work only when people are willing to co-operate for the common good. If they stand on prerogatives and forget responsibilities, the nation will quickly be paralyzed.

13

THE DUTY OF THE DEMOCRATIC PARTY

I believe that the American people have had their fill of partisanship just for the sake of partisanship; that they have had enough of opposing just for opposition's sake. I believe that the people are no longer enchanted by the frivolity and the transparent theatrics and the silly showmanship which have been grafted on to the election process.

We offer ourselves—on our record and by our platform—as a party for all Americans. This prosperous people, this land of reasonable men, has no place for petty partisanship or peevish prejudice. The needs of all can never be met by parties of the few. The needs of all cannot be met by a business party or a labor party, not by a war party or a peace party, not by a Southern party or a Northern party.

We are citizens of the oldest democracy on earth. We are members of the oldest political party in the world.

When our country and our party began, some of the wisest men of the age predicted that this light of freedom—the Great American Experiment— would soon be extinguished. They were wrong. The democratic idea of self-government has proved to be the most powerful political idea ever to stir the imagination of human beings.

Our party has greatly contributed to the success of the American Experiment. We have never represented a single interest; we have never represented a single group; we have never represented a single section of the country. The Democratic Party has endured and prospered because it rested on the belief that a party exists to advance the freedom and the welfare of all the people.

When Franklin Delano Roosevelt was suddenly succeeded by Harry Truman, the Nation did not falter. Both men had deep and abiding local attachments. Both men respected legitimate local interests. But both men also affirmed that the national interest is greater than the sum of all local interests.

John F. Kennedy was taken suddenly from us, deprived by an assassin of the chance to lead his party and his nation. But the principles and the purposes for which he labored continue to live. Our system of government was shocked but not paralyzed, and it began quickly to move again toward the high goals of America's destiny.

This continuity of purpose—from man to man, from administration to administration—is the secret of our strength as a party. A generation ago Franklin Roosevelt said that the world must be founded on four freedoms—freedom of speech, freedom of worship, freedom from want, and freedom from fear. When Roosevelt spoke, only a few nations in the world enjoyed those freedoms. A generation later, due in great measure to American leadership, those same freedoms flourish in many other parts of the world. Here at home, efforts to restrict our own freedoms have been consistently defeated.

We are not a foreign policy or a domestic policy party. As the party of all of the people, Democrats are dedicated to doing all the work that the well-being of our people may require, whether it is at home or abroad.